"To practice any art,
no matter how well or badly,
is a way to make
your soul grow.
So do it."

-Kurt Vonnegut

Coloring Test Page

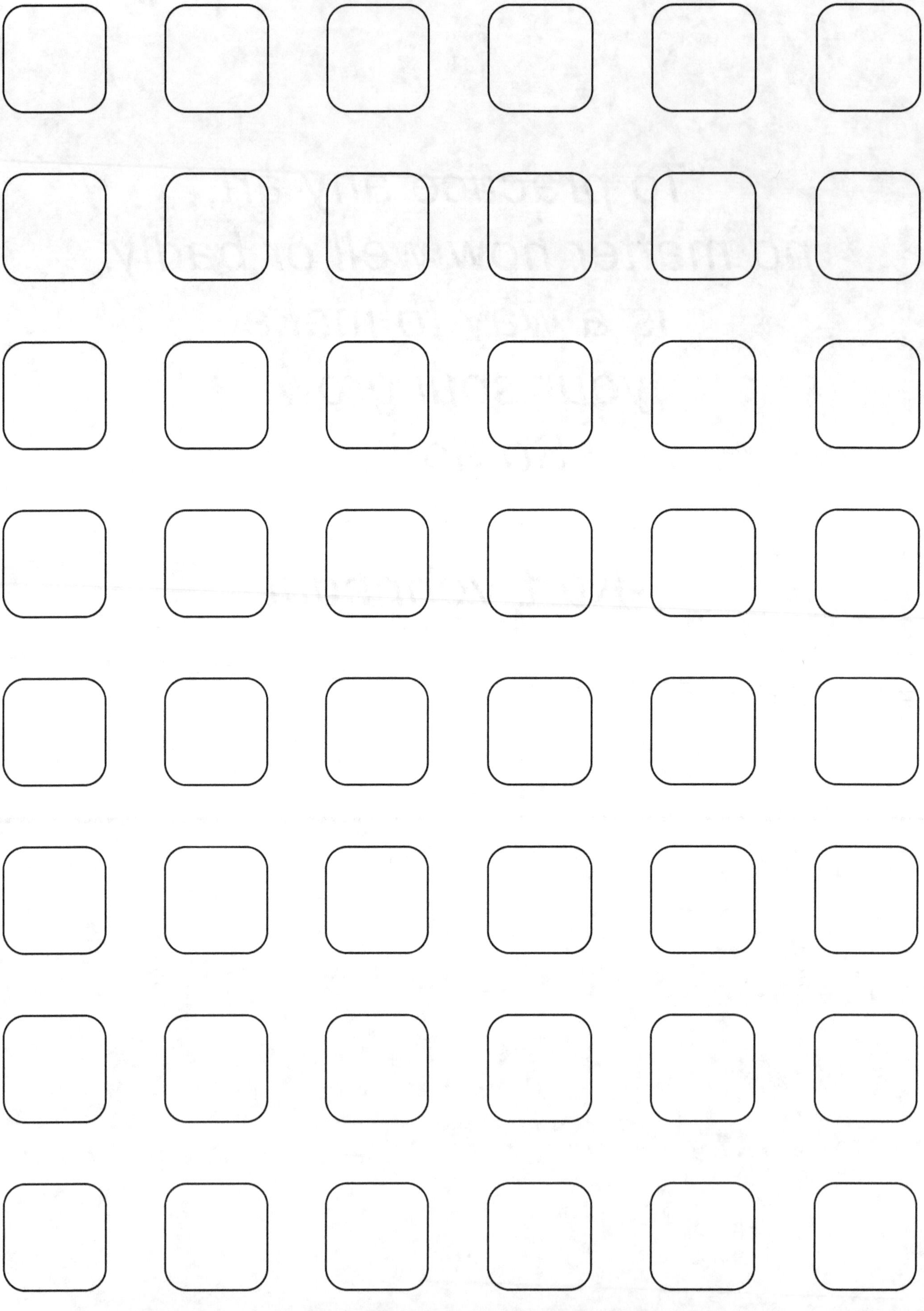

Coloring Test Page

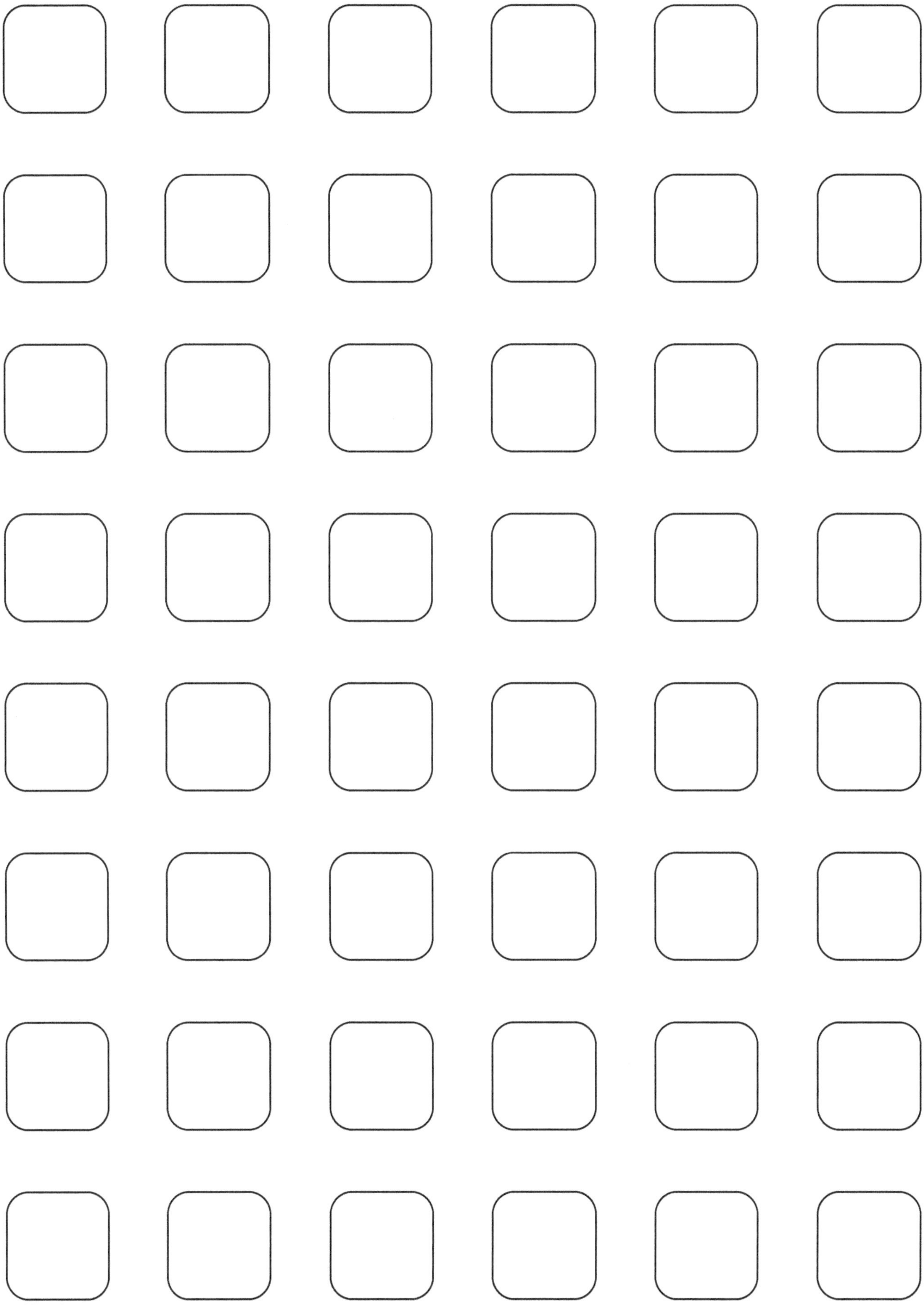

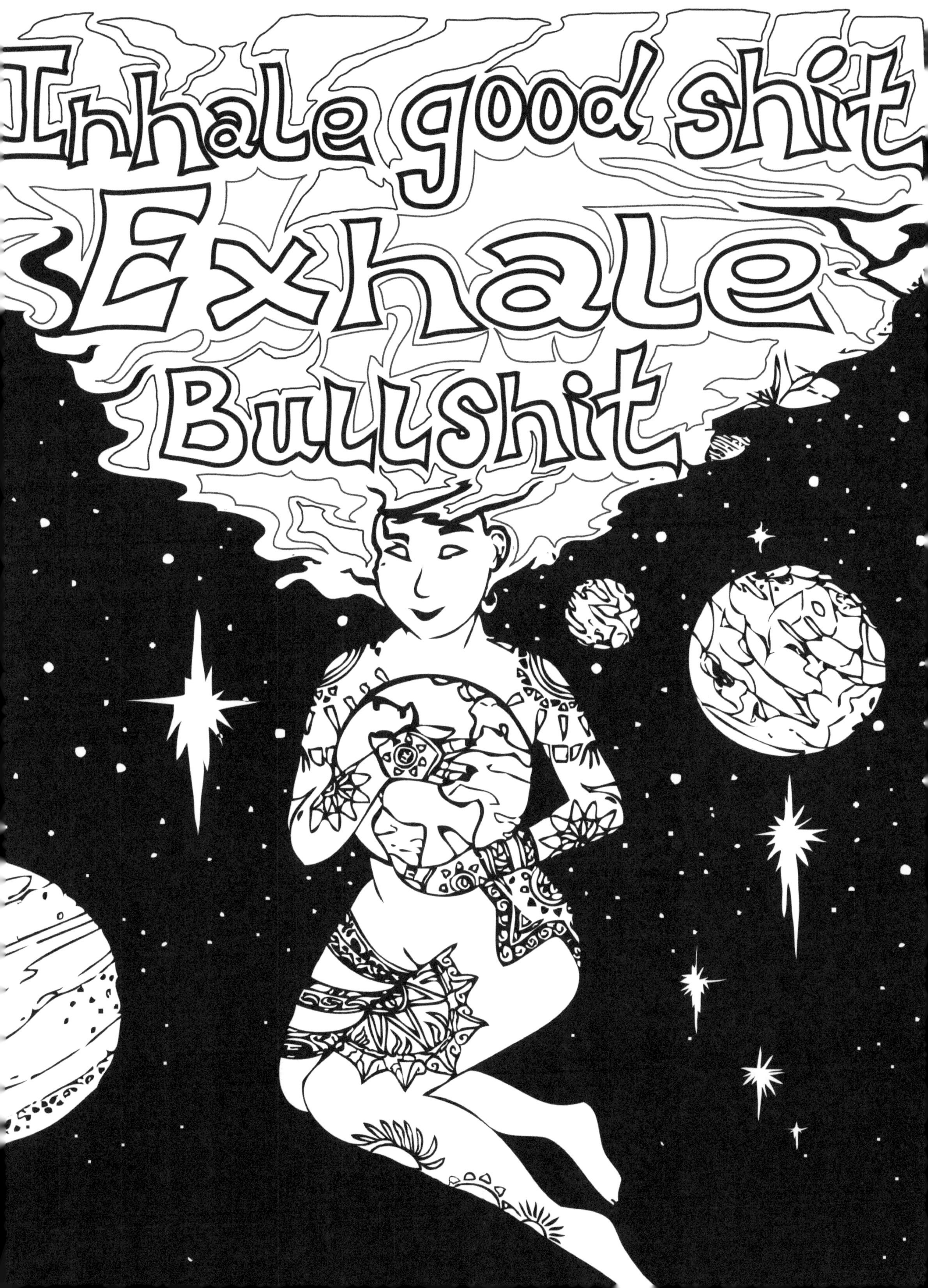
Inhale good shit
Exhale
Bullshit

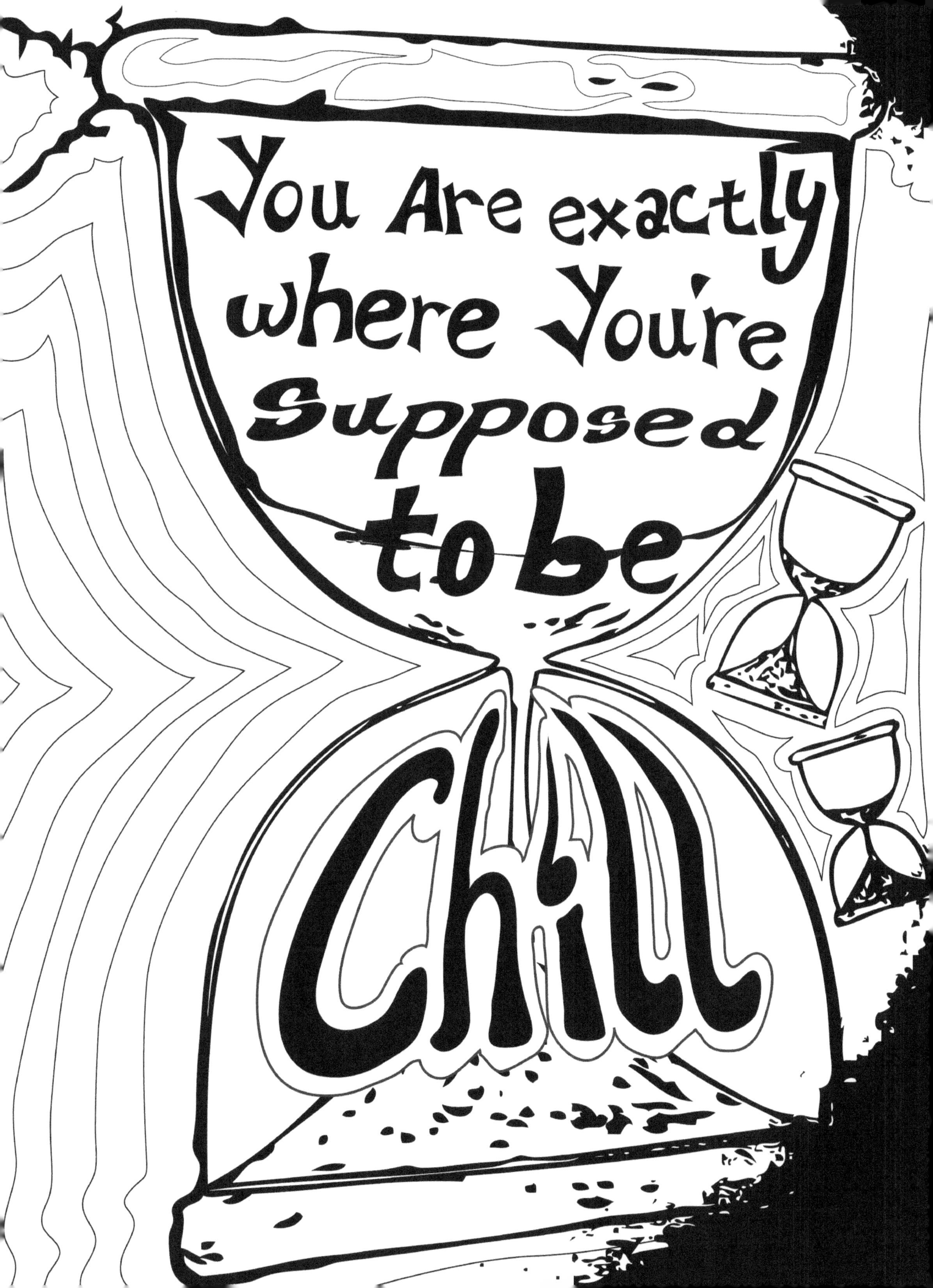
You Are exactly
where You're
Supposed
to be
Chill

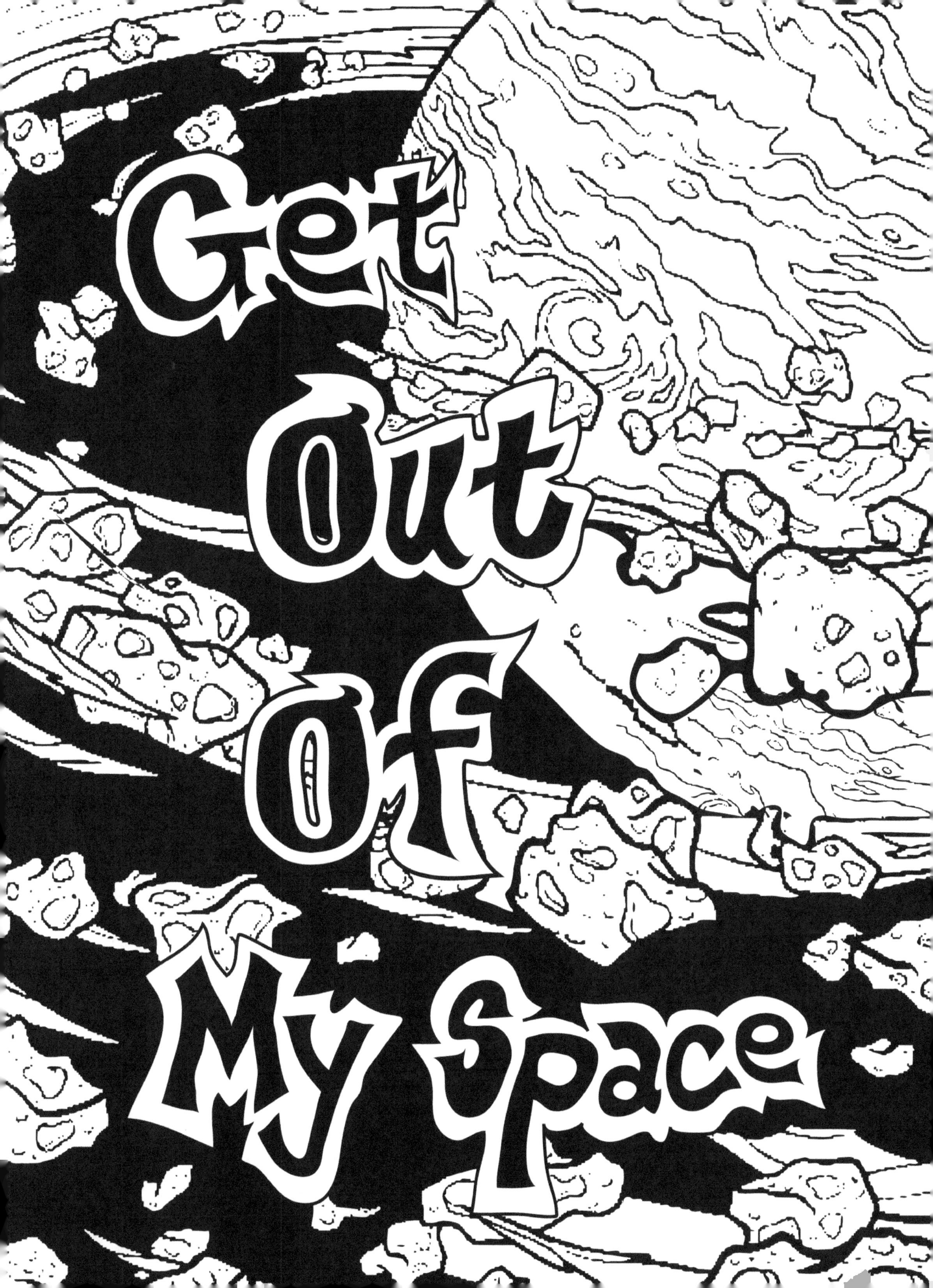
Get
Out
Of
My Space

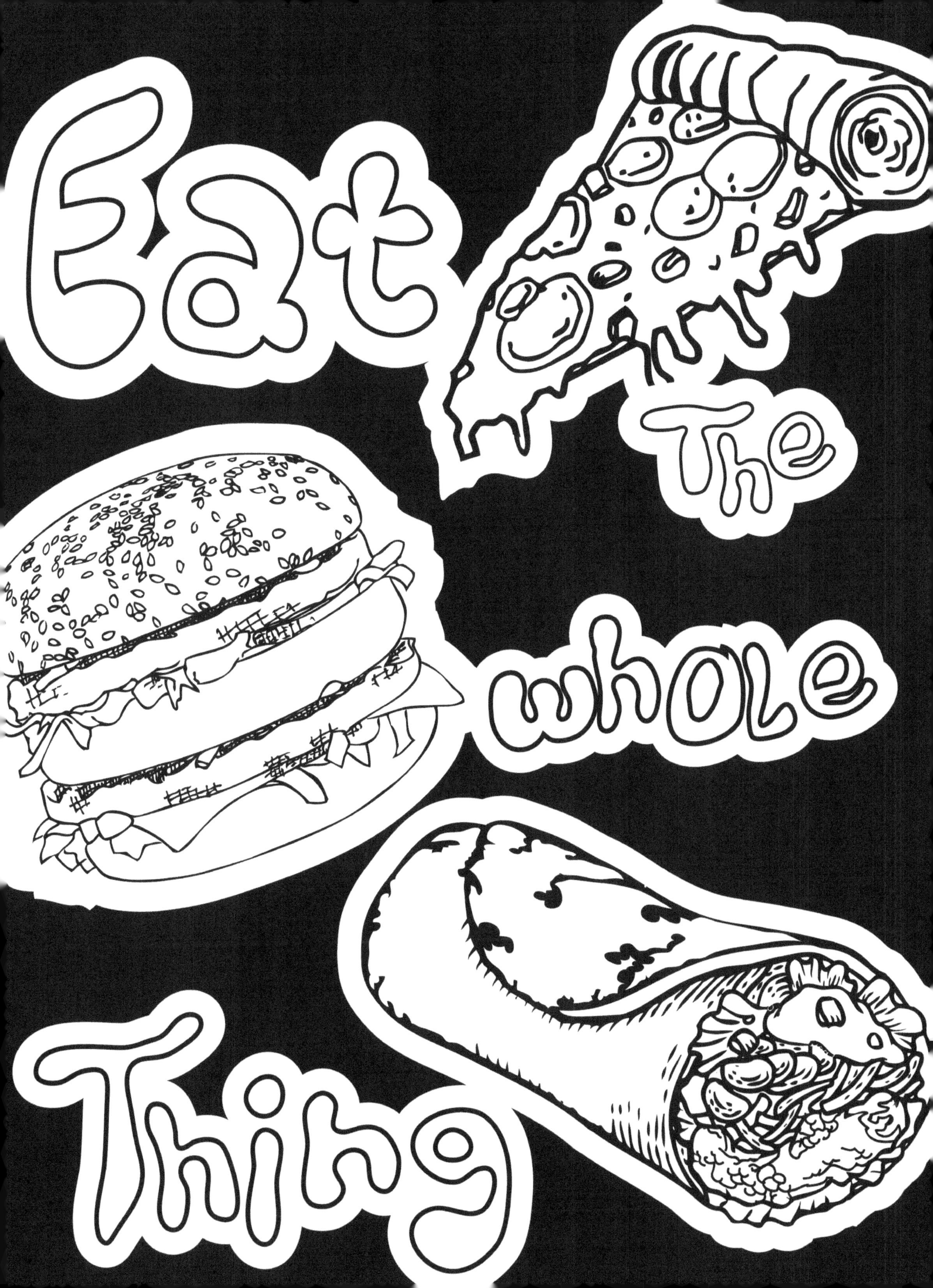
Eat
The
whole
Thing

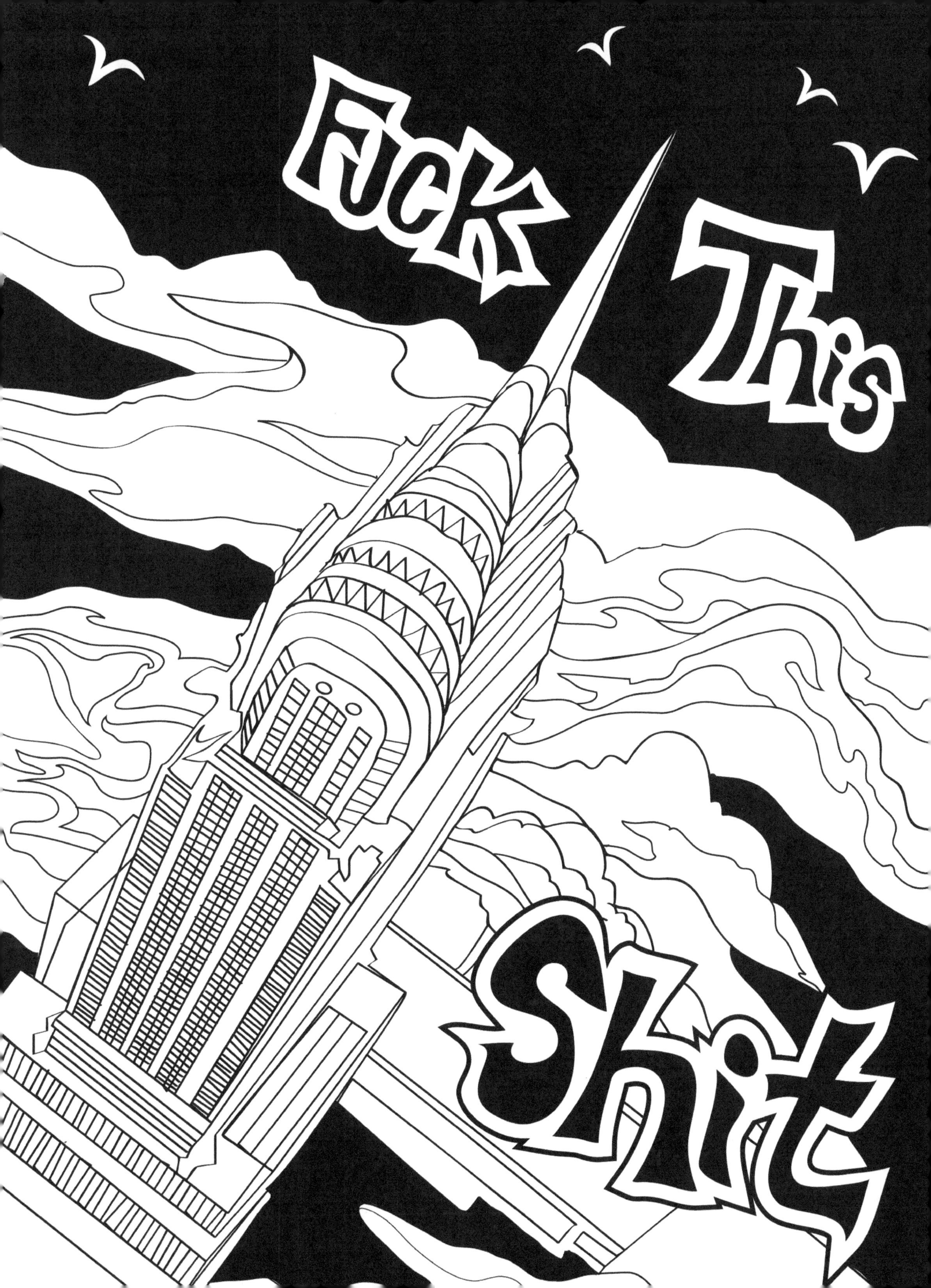
Fuck This
Shit

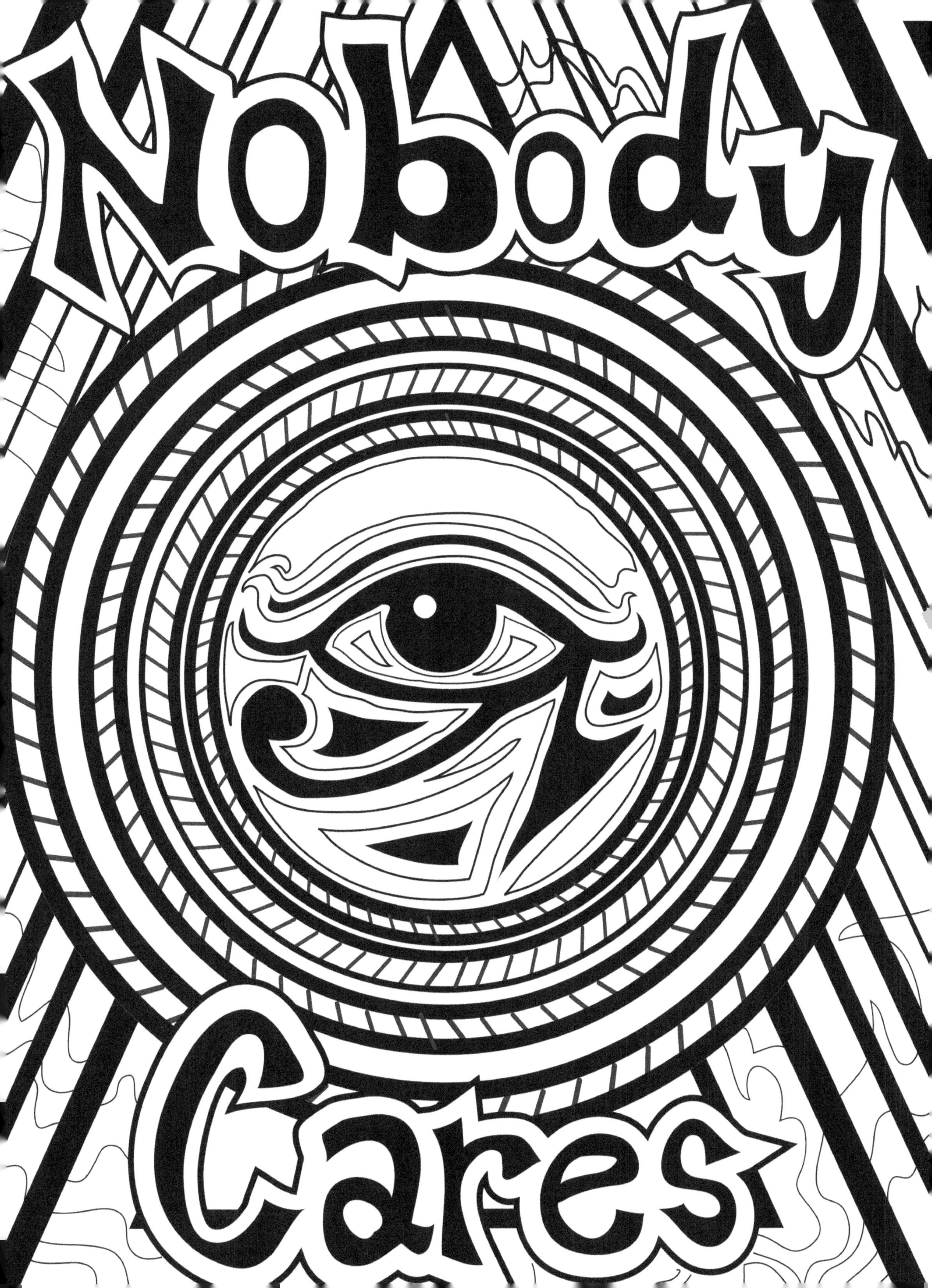
Nobody
Cares

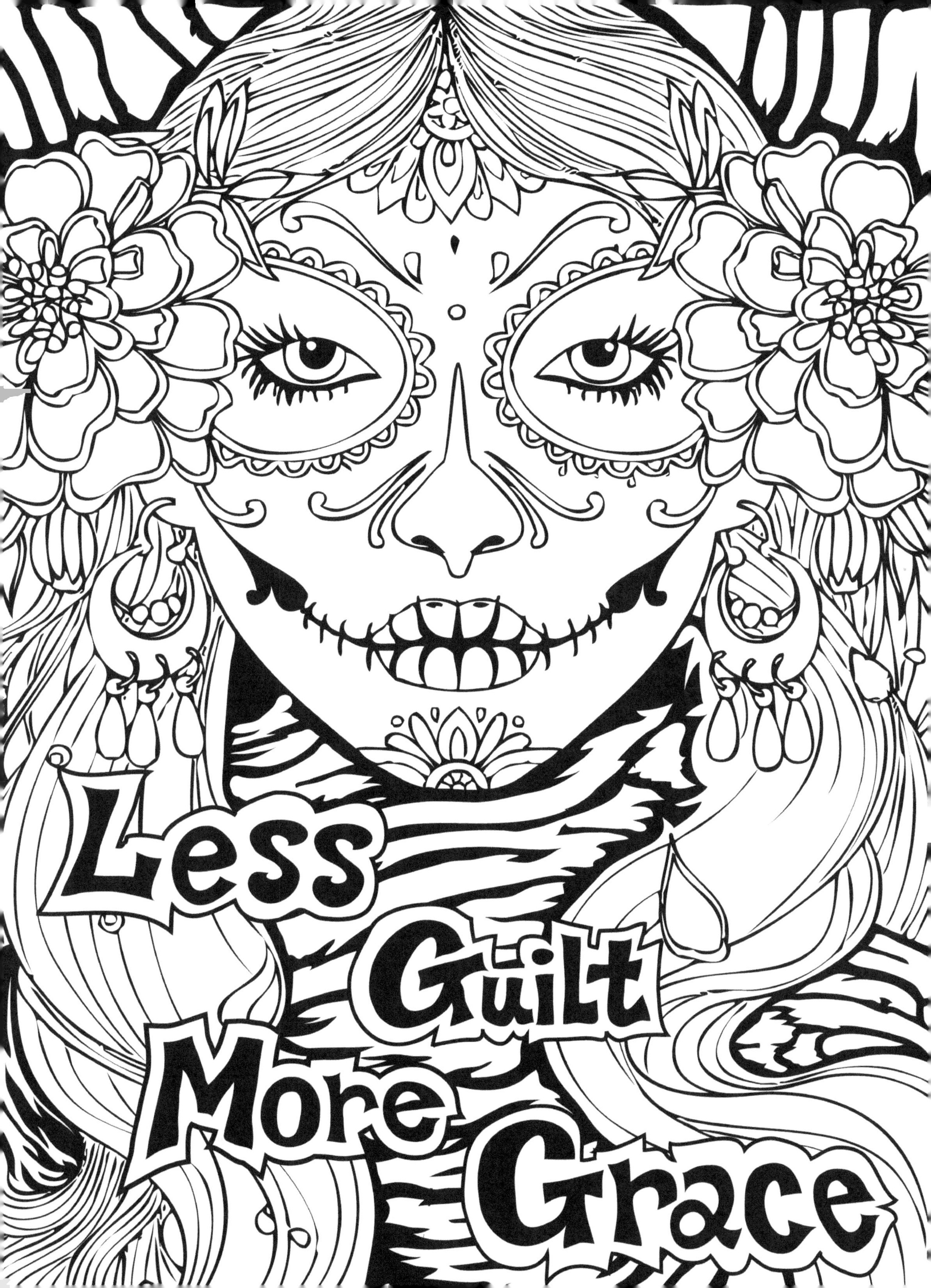
Less
Guilt
More
Grace

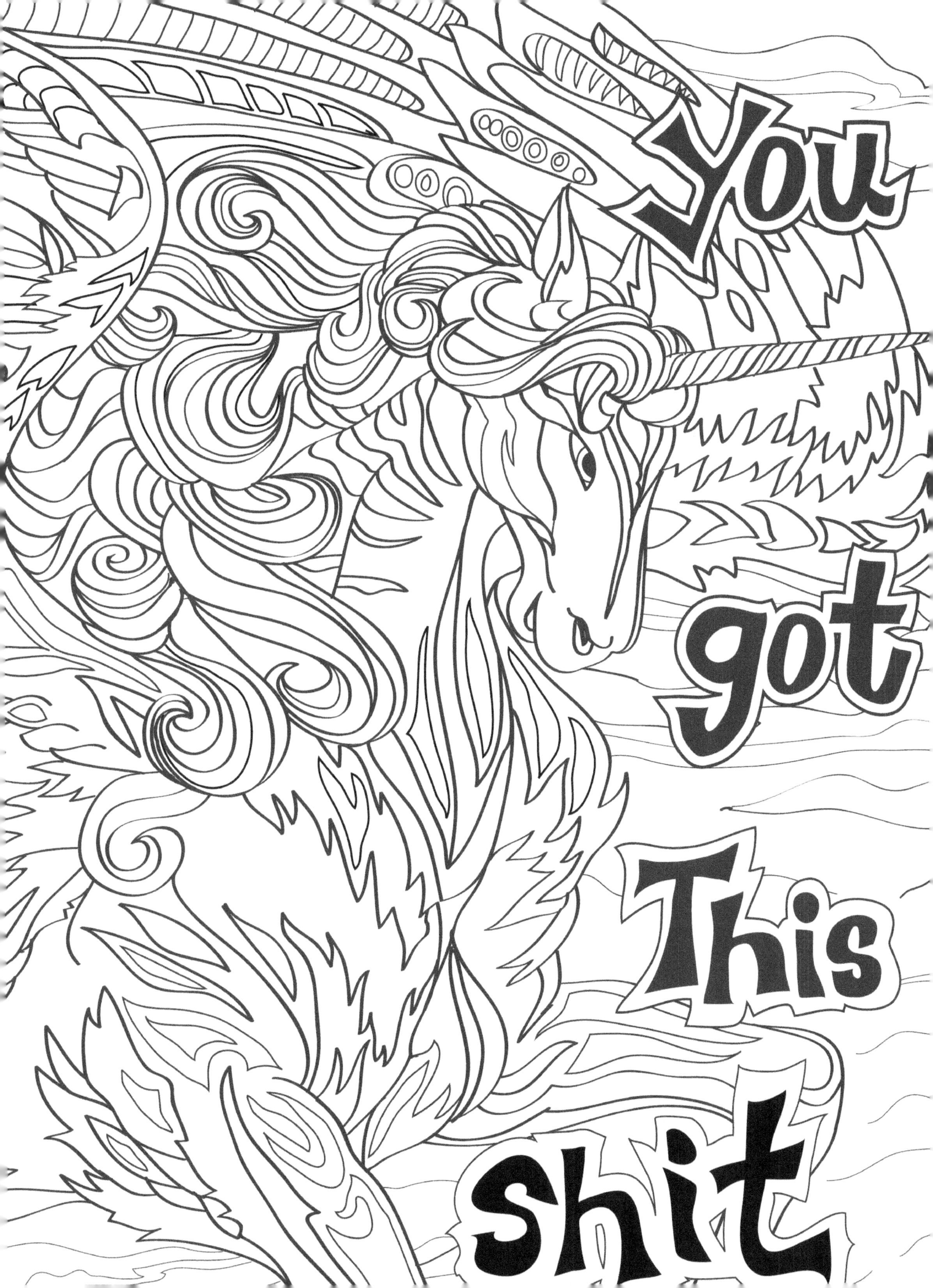
You
got
This
Shit

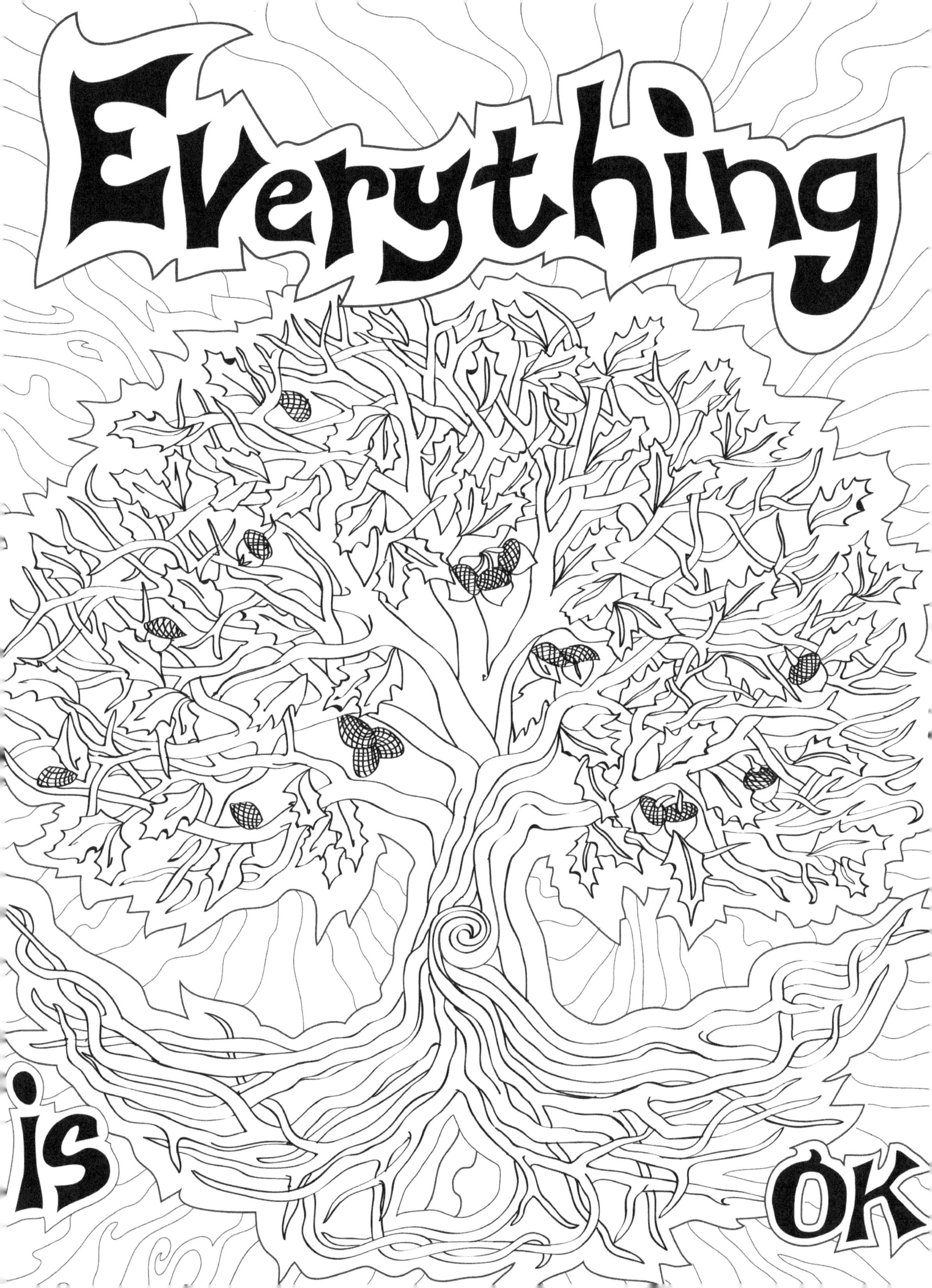
Everything
is
OK

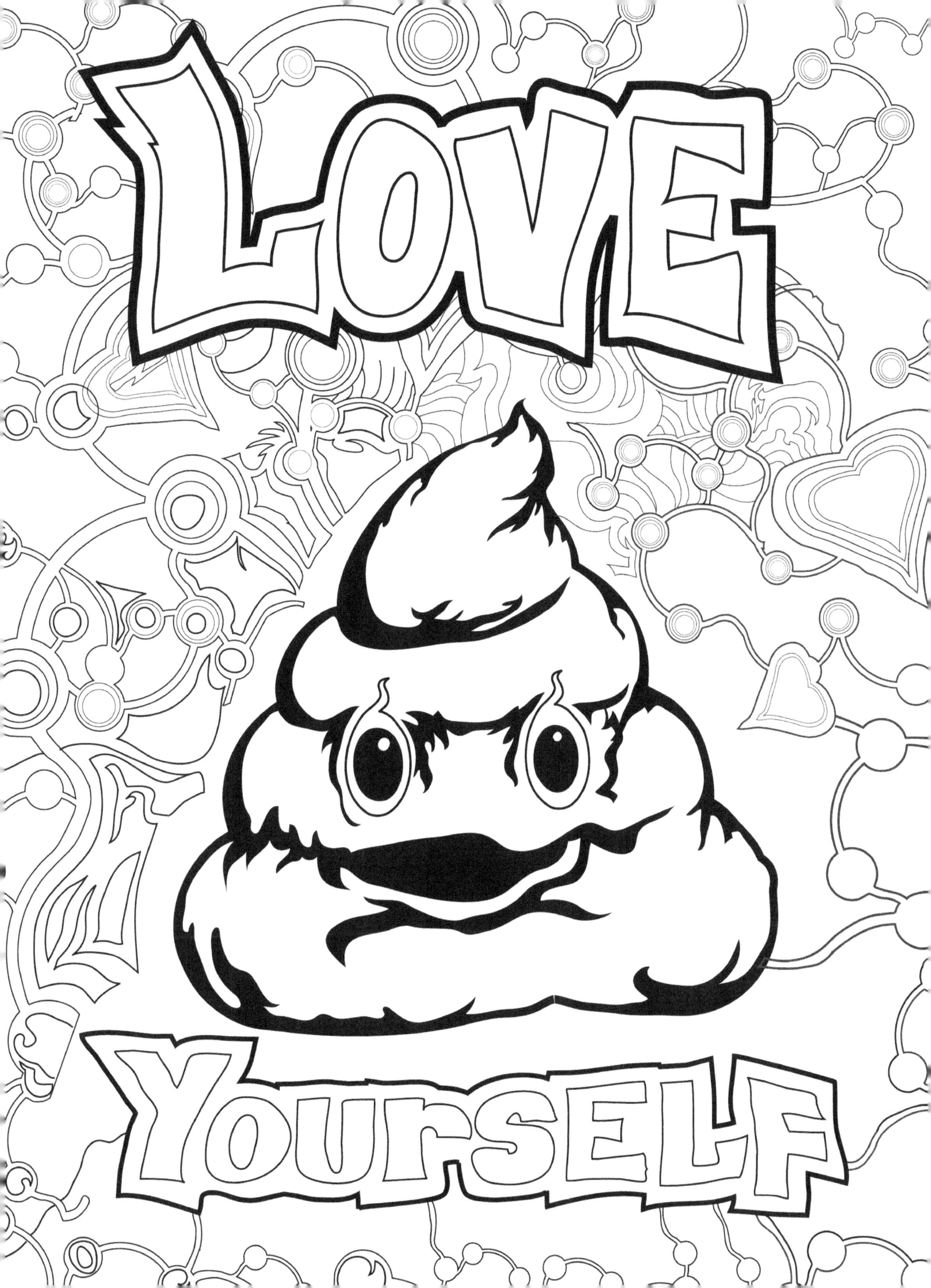
LOVE
YOURSELF

www.ingramcontent.com/pod-product-compliance
Lightning Source LLC
Chambersburg PA
CBHW080534190526
45169CB00008B/3161
* 9 7 8 1 5 3 2 3 9 9 1 1 4 *